Max a

Other Hopscotch books

THE ADVENTURES OF BLUNTER BUTTON *Phyllis Arkle*
WILLIAM WART-HOG, ZOO-KEEPER *Lindsey Chappell*
STRANGE HILL *Mary Cockett*
THE SIGN OF THE SMILING LION *Peter J. Davies*
ARTHUR'S FUNNY BIRTHDAY *Sophie Davis*
SAM THE SILVER BUS *Joan Eadington*
SAM'S WONDERFUL WEEK *Joan Eadington*
BAXTER BY THE SEA *Anne Forsyth*
TOO MANY GRANS! *Griselda Gifford*
GEMMA AND THE WITCH'S HOUSE *Pamela Gilbert*
MERMAN IN MAIDS MORETON *Jane Holiday*
IT'S TOO FRIGHTENING FOR ME *Shirley Hughes*
KING OF THE KNOCKDOWN GINGERS *Geraldine Kaye*
THE SKY-BLUE DRAGON *Geraldine Kaye*
THE SCHOOL POOL GANG *Geraldine Kaye*
BIM, THE VERY SPECIAL BEAR *Frances Lindsay*
GRIMBLEGRAW AND THE WUTHERING WITCH *Barbara Sleigh*
FANNY WITCH AND THE THUNDER LIZARD *Jeremy Strong*
DRAGONS LIVE FOREVER *Robert Swindells*
CHANGING OF THE GUARD *H. E. Todd*
LILY LOSES HER LOLLIPOP *Diana Webb*
SECRET WITCH *Robina Beckles Willson*
HOLIDAY WITCH *Robina Beckles Willson*
SPORTY WITCH *Robina Beckles Willson*
THE JUNGLE SNOWMEN *Caroline Wylie*
THE JUNGLE STORM *Caroline Wylie*
THE BROKEN TAMBOURINE *Nick Yapp*

and many other titles

Max and the Birthday Bat

Eleanor Allen

Illustrated by Janina Ede

HODDER AND STOUGHTON
LONDON SYDNEY AUCKLAND TORONTO

British Library Cataloguing in Publication Data

Allen, Eleanor
Max and the birthday bat.—(Hopscotch)
I. Title II. Ede, Janina
823'.914[J] PZ7

ISBN 0-340-40544-9

First published 1987

Published by Hodder and Stoughton Children's Books, a division of Hodder and Stoughton Ltd, Mill Road, Dunton Green, Sevenoaks, Kent TN13 2YJ

Photoset by Rowland Phototypesetting Ltd, Bury St Edmunds, Suffolk

Printed in Great Britain by St Edmundsbury Press Ltd, Bury St Edmunds, Suffolk

The very first bats Max saw were stuffed ones. They were on display in a big glass case in the local museum, above the library.

Max usually went up to the museum for a look around after he had chosen his library books. It was only a small museum, but it was crammed with interesting exhibits. Max's favourites were a glass case full of model dinosaurs and one with a real, stuffed, snarling fox. He always went to stare at the dinosaurs first, then at the fox – until the day he discovered the case of bats, that is. Then the order changed. Bats came first. In fact, the dinosaurs and the fox hardly got a look in any more. Max was completely hooked on BATS!

'Look at their sharp little teeth,' said Max to his mum one day, when she came to drag him away.

'Mmm . . . I wouldn't fancy a nip from those, would you?' cringed Mum.

'And look at that one with its wings spread out like it's flying. What are bats' wings made of? What do they feel like?'

Max pressed his nose against the case. He would love to touch a bat. He would love to stroke its furry body and examine the texture of its wings. He could imagine one hanging from his outstretched finger. His own bat. A pet bat.

'I wish I had a bat of my own,' said Max.

Mum snorted. 'Whatever for? They make me cringe. I think about witches and haunted houses and graveyards. You can hardly call them cuddly.'

'Well, I think they're cuddly,' said Max. 'I want a bat.'

'You know it's my birthday soon,' said Max to his dad that evening. 'Well, I've been thinking . . .'

Dad's hands tightened on his newspaper. 'Yee . . . es?' he said, hesitantly. Dad knew what was coming –

he was going to be asked for a present. He wondered what it would be, and picked through the possibilities in his mind.

If it was a pair of roller skates Max wanted, no problem.

If it was a Transformer – well, he could afford one, provided it wasn't Optimus Prime . . .

On the other hand, it might be a BMX bike – then there'd be trouble! No way, thought Dad, can I afford a BMX bike!

'Can I have a bat?' asked Max.

'A – oh, a bat? A BAT?' Dad gave an enormous sigh of relief and laid down his newspaper. A bat – that was even simpler than he'd hoped.

Dad wrapped Max in a warm, encouraging smile.

'Of course you can have a bat, son! Tell you what, we'll go and look at some tomorrow, shall we? Woolies have got some nice strong ones, not too dear.'

'Woolies?' repeated Max in some surprise. 'Do you mean you can get bats at Woolies?' He knew Woolworth's sold an awful lot of different things, but he'd never seen anything live for sale in there.

'Do you have to order them?' he asked.

'Course not,' said Dad. 'You can just pick them off the shelf.'

As Max stood puzzling that out, his mum came in.

'Guess what – Max wants a bat for his birthday,' Dad announced cheerfully and drove an imaginary cricket ball across the carpet.

Mum looked at Dad, then she looked at Max, and then she burst out laughing.

'Wrong bat, I'm afraid,' she said. 'I think he means a live one – you know, the sort that hangs upside down and catches insects.'

When Dad had got over this surprise and disappointment at being asked for a live bat and not a cricket bat, he put on a 'let's be reasonable about this' face.

'No point in beating about the bush,' he said. 'I'll tell you straight, son – you can't buy bats at a pet shop. As far as I know, you can't buy bats anywhere – they're becoming so rare these days, they've had to be specially protected by the law. You'll just have to settle for a nice pair of roller skates instead.'

The following week Max and his mum went to the library again to change their books. Afterwards they went to visit the bat case in the museum. But for once Max didn't want to hang about. He was eager to get home and read his new library books because every one of those books was about bats.

Max had thought of a plan. Maybe you couldn't buy a bat, but there was nothing to stop you FINDING one.

Max learned all sorts of things about bats from his books. Most important, he learned where they live. He made a list of

their favourite places: caves; hollow trees; old farm buildings; the attics of ordinary houses.

There were no caves near Max's house, so he crossed that off straight away.

Hollow trees . . . Well, there was one hollow tree he could think of, on the common. That would be worth a try.

Old farm buildings . . . Yes, his friend Mr McFarlane had a farm with some old buildings. He could try those.

Ordinary houses . . . Max's house was an ordinary house. Supposing he had bats living there already – a whole colony of them maybe, hanging from the rafters in the dusty, disused space above his bed?

That night Max lay awake listening extra hard for scuffling sounds and squeakings and the flapping of wings, but the only sound of wildlife he heard was the caterwauling of next door's cat.

He parted his curtains so that he could stare up at the night sky, but no dark bat-shapes flitted across the moon's bright face . . .

'You haven't put Micky's travelling basket back in the attic yet, Mum,' said Max next morning. The cat's basket still stood in the hall where they'd left it after his trip to the vet's. Max gave it a kick. 'It's getting in everybody's way!' he complained.

'Is it?' said Mum. 'I'll put it back when I get round to it.'

'Can I put it back?' asked Max. 'Now?'

'You?' Mum laughed off the suggestion. 'You couldn't climb a steep ladder carrying a heavy basket.'

'I've never seen in the attic,' said Max.

Mum shot him a suspicious look. 'Why do you want to see the attic?'

'I was wondering,' said Max, 'if there are any bats up there.'

'I doubt it,' said Mum, 'but we'll have a look when I've finished the washing-up.'

Mum let Max hold the torch. He shone it over cardboard boxes full of old letters

and papers; over a little chest of drawers that used to be in his room before he got a new one; over his baby-bath and cot that somebody else might need some day . . .

then he shone the torch over the rafters. The attic was dark and quiet and very spooky. Max didn't like it much. It seemed a perfect place for bats, but nowhere in Max's attic was a single bat to be found.

Downstairs again, Max crossed attics off his list.

'Can we fly my kite, up on the common?' Max asked his dad the following afternoon.

Dad shuffled impatiently. He was watching snooker on TV. 'OK – but not till I've finished watching this,' he agreed reluctantly.

It was perfect kite-flying weather, but of course Max's mind wasn't really on kites. He was thinking about the hollow tree that stood near the edge of the common. It was a very big tree and it reminded Max of drawings he'd seen where trees looked like people. The spreading branches were its arms; the

twisted roots its legs and the black hollow was like an open, shouting mouth.

'Will you give me a leg-up, so I can see what's inside that hollow tree?' Max asked his dad. 'I think there might be some bats living in there.'

'Shouldn't think so,' said Dad, but he helped Max up anyway.

Only a second or two passed before Max scrambled down again.

'Well?' said Dad. 'See any bats?'

Max shook his head. He looked both sad and angry at the same time. 'It's all black and sooty inside,' he said, 'like somebody lit a fire in it. And there's nothing but rubbish there – an empty crisp packet and a squashed Coke tin and some crumpled-up newspaper. No bats would want to live there now.'

When he got home, Max crossed the hollow tree off his list.

A day or two passed before Max spotted Mr McFarlane standing in his

farmyard. Max was on his way home from school with his mum.

'Hello, Mr McFarlane,' he called.

'Hello, Max. Been to school? Get all your sums right?'

'No,' frowned Max. 'I got two wrong. Have you got any bats in your old farm buildings, please?'

'It's his new craze,' said Mum, tapping her forehead. 'Bat mad! He's got bats in the belfry, I'm afraid.'

Mr McFarlane rubbed his chin thoughtfully. 'We used to have dozens,' he said. 'But you don't see many these days – all the pesticides are killing them

off. Let's think – we used to have a few in the dovecote. Want to look?'

Mum went into the farmhouse for a cup of tea with Mrs McFarlane. Max followed the farmer to a strange little tower-shaped building with a very low and narrow wooden door.

'Is this a dovecote?' he asked. 'What's it for?'

'It's a special house for doves or pigeons,' said the farmer. 'They used to keep flocks of birds in the past. They collected the eggs and ate the birds in winter when they'd no other meat. Most dovecotes are empty now, like mine, but they're unusual buildings and worth keeping.'

Mr McFarlane turned the big rusty key and stooped to the little door. 'If I get stuck,' he laughed, 'just give my backside a push!'

For a minute or two, Max forgot about bats as he stared around Mr McFarlane's dovecote. It was almost dark, but not quite because rays of light were slanting through an opening at the top. All around the walls were row upon row of holes where the birds could nest. There were five hundred and fifty holes altogether and each hole could take a pair of birds. In the middle there was a long, slender, wooden ladder attached to a post. You could swing the ladder round to reach every hole. Mr McFarlane let Max stand on the ladder and gave him a ride. Max thought the dovecote was the most mysterious and magical place he had ever been into.

Unfortunately, not only weren't there any doves or pigeons in there any more, there were no bats either. For some reason, all the bats had gone.

Sadly, Max crossed old farm buildings off his list too.

Max's birthday was very near by now, and still he hadn't found a bat. What's more, he'd run out of places to look – except belfries, of course. Max hadn't put those on his list because people always laughed about bats in belfries and he thought it might only be a joke. He wouldn't have bothered with belfries at all but just by chance, on the day before his

birthday, his mother decided to visit old Mrs Cotgreave who lived in a cottage by the church.

Mrs Cotgreave's cottage had a very big garden and soon Max was sent out to play in it. Within seconds he had crawled through a hole in the hedge and stood staring up at the church tower.

Might there be bats up there?

Max tried the church door and found it opened. Cautiously he stepped inside. It was warm and welcoming inside the church, full of coloured patterns of light and the scent of polish and flowers.

He found the door to the tower and tried it, and that was unlocked too. Up the twisting stairs he crept. It wouldn't take long to check out the belfry and then he would come straight down again. And maybe when he came down, he

might be carefully carrying a bat.

Max reached the small, plain room where the heavy bellropes hung. The belfry was above, reached by climbing up a stout wooden ladder. Up he went and scrambled through the ladder opening on to a wooden platform. There he steadied himself and glanced curiously around. The church bells were hanging there, big and round as witches' cauldrons and just as weighty, held by bolts the size of his fist. Max stared at the bells in open-mouthed fascination and felt a sudden twinge of guilt. He knew he shouldn't be there – a belfry was not a place for boys.

A sudden noise, a scratching and a fluttering sent Max flat against the wall. Something darted down out of the gloom of the ancient rafters and shot out like an arrow through the long window slit. It wasn't a bat – only a sparrow.

Max gazed after the bird and discovered the view. He could see for miles, right over to the next village and the hills beyond. For a moment or two Max forgot all about bats as he crouched

beside the window, staring through.

Then, just as he was getting to his feet again, there came another noise. Heavy footsteps sounded. Somebody had come into the room below where the bell ropes hung! Very slowly Max lowered himself against the wall and tried to make himself as small as he could. He knew he would get into loads of trouble if he got caught up there!

Max dug his nails into the palms of his hands and waited for that person to go away. He waited and waited. But the person didn't go away. In fact, somebody else came up and joined him! Then somebody else, followed by somebody else. Footsteps echoed back and forth over the thick floorboards; people greeted each other; discussed the weather – it began to sound like a party was going on down there!

Max developed pins and needles in his feet and a crick in his neck. He felt more

than just uncomfortable – he felt screamingly uncomfortable. And he was anxious too. He wondered if his mum had gone to call him in from Mrs Cotgreave's garden yet . . .

Suddenly there was a great deal of throat-clearing. Then – silence . . .

Max breathed a deep, soft sigh of relief. They're going, he thought, at last . . .!

BOOM! CLANG! BOOM!

Max shook from head to foot – the whole tower shook with him. Sound pierced his ears like jagged lightning as the great bells swung.

In a blind panic Max flung himself at the opening, grappling with the ladder. In his haste, his feet slipped. He clung on with his hands, but his legs waved helplessly about in space.

The bells stopped ringing as suddenly as they'd started. A babble of voices began shouting things like 'There's a lad up there!' 'Grab him – quick before he falls!' and 'The stupid little blighter!'

Firm, large hands grasped Max about his waist. He struggled and kicked, but the hands didn't let go. They hauled him down the ladder and sat him in the middle of the dusty floor.

Fearfully Max looked up into the circle of bellringers' faces and he wished he could disappear through a crack in the floor.

'Well, well,' said one, 'I've heard of BATS in belfries – but never BOYS in belfries! What were you doing up there, Sonny-Jim?'

'Bats,' stammered Max. 'That's what I was looking for – bats.' And he choked back a torrent of tears. 'You won't tell my mum, will you?'

'Bats?' The man who had helped Max down stared hard at him. 'Why were you looking for bats, hey?' he asked sternly.

'I like them,' sniffed Max. 'I wanted one for my birthday. But my dad says you can't buy one, and I can't find one anywhere 'cos all the pesticides are killing them off.'

'That's right,' said the man. 'And supposing you'd found a bat – what were you going to do with it?'

'I was going to take it home and look after it.'

'And where were you going to keep it?'

Max looked blank.

'You hadn't thought of that, had you, hey?'

Max bit his lip. 'No,' he admitted reluctantly, 'I don't think I had.'

'You can't keep bats as pets, you know,' said the man. 'They're becoming so rare, the Government has had to make some special laws to protect them. It's against the law to disturb a bat – it's even against the law to TOUCH one – unless you've got a special licence. Have you got a special licence?'

Silently Max shook his head.

'I thought not.'

The man frowned at him so hard that Max realised intending to touch a bat was just as bad as actually touching one. 'I'm sorry,' he said.

The man's face became a little friendlier. 'All right then, I'll tell you what – if you're really interested in bats – interested in protecting and preserving them, that is, it could be that, in a roundabout way, you've come to the right place.'

'You mean there ARE some bats in the belfry?' cried Max.

'No.' The man (whose name was Mr Jones) shook his head. 'That's not what I mean at all,' he said mysteriously.

Mr Jones took Max back to his mum – and golly, was Mum cross when she heard about his exploits!

'But don't be too hard on him,' urged Mr Jones. 'No harm was done. And I can sympathise with the lad. I'm a bat enthusiast myself. I'm secretary of the local Bat Group.'

'I didn't know there was such a thing,' said Mum.

'A word in your ear,' said Mr Jones. He took Mum aside and had what appeared to be a very serious word indeed with her.

Max felt full of foreboding. He was sure that when his dad came home that evening there'd be worse tellings-off in store.

But, in actual fact, the worse tellings-off never came. Maybe, thought Max, it's because of my birthday.

The very next day was the birthday itself. Before he went to school Max opened his cards and a present which contained a pair of smart red roller skates. The skates were very nice, but it's hard to get enthusiastic about roller skates when what you really wanted was a bat.

'You can open your other presents tonight,' said Mum. 'And there'll be a special one, but it hasn't arrived yet.'

'Well I know what it's not,' said Max mournfully. 'It's not a bat.'

'No,' said Mum. 'It couldn't be a bat, could it? But I promise you, it's something just as good.'

Nothing, thought Max dejectedly, could be just as good as a bat.

At school that day Max drew a whole page of bats in his special interest book.

'It's come!' said Mum excitedly when she collected Max from school.

'What has?'

'Your special present.'

'What is it?'

'Wait and see.'

When they got home Mum led Max through into the back garden and pointed with a flourish. 'Happy birthday, Max!'

A plain wooden box was lying on the lawn.

Max looked at the box, then he looked at his mum and wondered if she was feeling all right. 'It's just a box!'

'No – you're wrong. Go and look.'

Max went over and examined the box. It had a narrow slit underneath and an envelope addressed to him on top. He took the envelope and opened it and read the note inside. Then slowly a smile spread across his face until it reached from ear to ear.

'Well?' asked Mum. 'What does it say?'

'It says, "Get your dad to fix this box high up on a south-facing wall of your house and I hope you'll soon have some

occupants. Happy birthday, Max, from Mr Jones and the Bat Group." It's a BAT BOX!'

'Is it a good present?'

'Fantastic!'

'I told you it would be just as good as actually having a bat.'

'It's even better! I might get more than one. I think there's room for a whole bat family in here . . . '

'You realise you won't be able to touch them, only look? They won't be pets . . .'

Max nodded gravely. Mr Jones had explained all about that yesterday. He'd felt disappointed, but he'd understood. 'But I'll know they're there and that they're safe,' he said. 'And that's what really matters, isn't it . . .? I wonder when they'll come?'

'Not overnight,' Mum pointed out. 'You might have to be patient for a while.'

'Do you really think I'll get some?'

'If you're lucky.'

A few weeks later some little pipistrelle bats, looking for a safe, vacant, roosting

place, spotted Max's box and decided to make their home in it, quite close to his bedroom window. As he sat up in bed, watching their dark shapes flitting soundlessly across his garden, Max didn't just feel lucky – he felt very, very proud.